Chri

to Sarah and Rod —
 Don't forget to come back;
in the meantime, don't forget
what it's like!

 Iris and Bonny

TWIN CITIES
MINNEAPOLIS-ST. PAUL
A PICTURE BOOK TO REMEMBER HER BY

Designed by
DAVID GIBBON

Produced by
TED SMART

CRESCENT BOOKS
NEW YORK

INTRODUCTION

Almost at the heart of the North American continent lies the state of Minnesota – 'Land of 10,000 Lakes' – as the licence plates on numerous automobiles proclaim, although there are in fact more than 15,000. The two most important cities, Minneapolis and St. Paul, ten miles apart on opposite banks of the Mississippi River, and containing two million inhabitants, about half the state's population, form the Twin Cities metropolitan area.

The history of Minneapolis dates back to the late 17th century when the territory was primarily occupied by two Red Indian tribes, the Chippewa and the Sioux. A Franciscan missionary, Father Louis Hennepin, visited the area in 1680 and named the Falls of St. Anthony, which were later to supply power for the earliest industry, saw milling, and subsequently for grinding flour for the first permanent U.S. settlement at Fort Snelling, a military outpost at the confluence of the Mississippi and Minnesota Rivers. The village of St. Anthony grew up on the eastern side of the falls and became incorporated in 1855.

European settlers, particularly Germans, Scandinavians and Irish, attracted by the vast forests of spruce, pine and balsam, illegally occupied military reservation land on the west side of the Mississippi, but in 1855 they were granted patent rights and the village of Minneapolis was incorporated a year later.

In 1860 St. Anthony was chartered as a city and Minneapolis acquired similar status in 1867. However, just five years later they merged into one under the name Minneapolis, which means 'water city'.

The site of St. Paul was largely ignored until the first land claim was made in 1838 by Pierre "Pig's Eye" Parrant. The settlement was known as Pig's Eye until 1841, when Father Lucian Galtier built a log chapel dedicated to St. Paul. In 1849 it became the capital of the newly-formed Minnesota Territory and, when the state was admitted into the Union in 1858, acquired the title State Capital.

The advance of the railroad in the 19th century benefited both Minneapolis and St. Paul. Connections were made with the south through Chicago, and with the east via Sault Sainte Marie. The rich wheatlands of the Red River valley and the Dakotas were opened up, with the result that Minneapolis became 'the flour city of the U.S.A.' Flour milling soon superseded lumbering as the most important industry and the last lumber mill closed in 1919. Other industries were developed in the 1880's such as agricultural and railroad machinery manufacture, as well as the extraction of linseed oil from flax that was grown locally.

Nearly 100 years later, Minneapolis is the largest city in Minnesota and, with St. Paul, a thriving commercial and industrial centre. It is also an impressive city with 156 beautiful parks and 22 lakes within the city limits. One of these, Lake Minnetonka, has an outlet, Minnehaha Creek, which flows eastwards and cascades 15 metres over an escarpment at Minnehaha Falls, immortalised as the "laughing water" in Henry Wadsworth Longfellow's epic poem "The Story of Hiawatha" (1855). A fine bronze statue of Hiawatha and Minnehaha stands above the falls; a tribute to the poet who, curiously, never set eyes on the famous location.

Minneapolis has twice been voted an 'All American City', its urban renewal programme, industrial development, low crime figures, lack of poverty and traffic congestion being greatly envied by other cities. To the visitor it emerges as truly cosmopolitan, with tremendous vitality and appreciation of culture and civic life. The Tyrone Guthrie Theatre is the home of one of the nation's leading repertory companies and the Minnesota Orchestra, one of the finest in the country, performs at Northrop Hall, University of Minnesota. A fine collection of modern American art can be seen at the Walker Art Centre, and fascinating exhibits at the Public Library's Science Museum and Planetarium.

For one week in July, the biggest summer festival in the United States, the Aquatennial, takes place, comprising more than 200 sports and entertainments. Yet all-year-round recreation is conveniently close. The unpolluted, fish-filled lakes are perfect for swimming, fishing, boating and water-skiing, and winter ski resorts are only a short drive away.

Although so close to each other, the Twin Cities are vastly different. Unlike Minneapolis, St. Paul is staid and conservative, with strong Irish-Catholic and Yankee influences and fervent pride in its architecture. In its early days its strategic position on the river bank ensured its importance as a trading post where goods such as furs and groceries were exchanged. The early industries, like boot and shoe making, were developed to satisfy the demands of the local population. When, in 1882, the Union Stock Yards Company was established by the railroads, it was the first step in making St. Paul one of the world's largest public livestock markets. The manufacture of automobiles, electronic equipment, beer and food products now predominate, and the city also has oil refineries, chemical plants and a steel mill. In addition, some of the largest corporations in the United States have their headquarters both here and in Minnesota.

At the end of January and the beginning of February, the Winter Carnival, St. Paul's answer to the Aquatennial, takes place. It includes national ski-jumping championships, cross-country ski races, ice-fishing contests and tobogganing down a slide in front of the State Capitol. The Snowmobile International "500" is also run; a race along a course between Winnipeg, Manitoba and St. Paul's itself. Snowmobiles have now become one of the most popular winter sporting vehicles, virtually replacing the dog sled, and they are used extensively in Minnesota's severe winters. Major league sports are also well represented in the Twin Cities, with the Vikings, North Stars, Twins, and St. Paul's Fighting Saints hockey team.

On a more cultural note, St. Paul has a Chamber Orchestra and Civic Opera Association of which they are justly proud. A new Arts and Science Centre and the well-stocked Como Zoo are two other attractions.

The University of Minnesota has a campus in both cities and its facilities are used not only by the descendents of those early European settlers but by the numerous Sioux and Chippewa who live in St. Paul and Minneapolis.

"Minnesota, Hats off to Thee" is a line from a rousing football song of the university. Not only could the words apply to the state as a whole, but particularly to the Twin Cities, where the quality of life is high and where there is respect for the past and careful consideration for the future.

A group of golden sculptured horses surmount the south entrance of Minnesota's majestic State Capitol, in St Paul, *left.*

Minneapolis, the great "All-American City", faces its "twin", St Paul, across the mighty Mississippi and together they form the industrial, educational and cultural hub of the northern Great Lakes region. This handsome city is characterised by an impressive skyline *above*, and seen *previous page* in a dramatic sunset; *left from* 3rd Avenue Bridge; *right* across the snow-bound Mississippi River, and *below*, a myriad twinkling lights beam out from the starkly-silhouetted high-rise buildings.

Home of the acclaimed Minnesota
Orchestra, seen in concert *above*
(photograph by courtesy of the Minnesot
Orchestral Association), Orchestra Hall
right is famous for its exciting design
concept and superior acoustics.

Sculpted by Raymond Duchamp-Villor
"Le Grand Cheval" shown *left* with
"Colonial Cubism" by Stuart Davies, and
"Damascus Stretch Variation" by Frank
Stella *below,* are part of the Walker Art
Center's extensive collection of
contemporary art.

As night enfolds the city, the glittering
Minneapolis skyline can be seen *overleaf*
from the junction of the I-94 and 280
freeways.

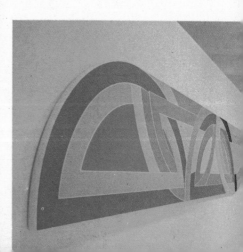

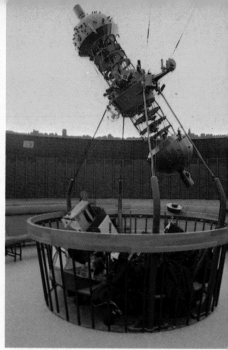

Considered to have the largest artistic
community between Minnesota and the
West Coast, the Twin Cities contain a
wealth of theatres, museums and cultural
institutions. Amongst the many fine
centres to be found in Minneapolis are:
The Guthrie Theater, the interior of which
is shown *above right,* a catalyst for the
metropolitan theatre community and said
to be the 'crown jewel' of the Twin Cities,
and the outstanding Science Museum, with
its beautifully displayed exhibits *centre
left,* fascinating Time and Space Gallery
below right, and exciting Planetarium
above. Top left can be seen the Public
Library and *bottom left* the superb interior
of the Auditorium, in the Convention
Center *below,* situated near the heart of
Downtown Minneapolis.

Soaring skyward, Minneapolis' tallest
building, the I.D.S. Center, is pictured
overleaf, with the Foshay Tower and
Orchestra Hall, in a winter landscape.

Around spacious, well-planned
Minneapolis a pleasing blend of
architectural styles mark the city's
distinctive skyline, seen over the St Paul
Freeway *right*. In the Downtown area
above left, the successful urban design of
the I.D.S. Center *below* dominates lovely
Nicollet Mall *left*, whilst Peavey Plaza
above provides a tranquil oasis in this
central business district. *Overleaf* is show
City Hall, flanked by the Bell Telephone
Building, overlooking Government Cente
Plaza.

Overlooking Government Plaza *below,*
City Hall *top right* is a major landmark of
Romanesque-revival architecture, and
within its foyer stands the superb statue of
the "Father of Waters" *centre right,* carved
in Florence in 1905 by Larken Goldsmith
Mead, from a single piece of Carrara
marble. *Above* is shown the magnificent
floodlit fountain in the foreground of the
Northwestern National Life Insurance
Building; *left and overleaf* beautiful
Loring Park, uniquely situated close to
bustling Downtown, and *bottom right* the
Mary Ruth Square Dancers performing in
Nicollet Mall.

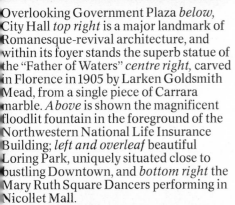

Throughout Minneapolis, innovative, contemporary design, as well as historic artistry, is evident in the widely differing architectural patterns that form the city skyline. Seen *left*, and across snow-banked Peavy Plaza *above*, the 775-foot high, glass-sheathed I.D.S. Tower exceeds the city's other lofty landmark, the Foshay Tower *below*, by 225 feet, whilst the mirrored Federal Reserve Bank Building *right* is actually suspended from a huge arch. Pictured *overleaf* is the stone built Wesley Church, Auditorium and Convention Hall.

Over 1,100 churches of various denominations, including the Westminster Presbyterian Church of Minneapolis, with its splendid interior *right,* serve the Twin Cities. Designed by Emmanuel L. Masqueray, the white granite Basilica of St Mary, in Minneapolis, *above left* is the Co-Cathedral of the Arch-diocese of Minneapolis and St Paul. A beautiful example of Modern Renaissance architecture, its massive square lantern-crowned dome is one of the Basilica's most striking features, and *left* is shown its magnificent, marble decorated interior.

Within the stately interior *above* of the Minneapolis Cathedral Church of St Mark can be seen the exquisite stained-glass Ascension Window, the first to be installed in the Church, above the graceful High Altar.

Against a darkening sky, the dramatic, rolling wave of Saint Anthony Falls, the unique Federal lock and dam area which was the lumbering and milling power source for early Minneapolis, is shown *overleaf.*

epicting Minnesota's rich Swedish eritage, the elegantly appointed rooms *ese pages,* which are among the thirty-ree contained within the American wedish Institute, the former mansion ome of Swan J. Turnblad, reveal the social nd cultural artifacts that span over 150 ears of the Swedish experience in merica.

Equally as impressive by day, the foaming hite blanket of Saint Anthony Falls is own *overleaf.*

ited to the south of the town, Lake
Nokomis *these pages*, is one of twenty-two
sparkling lakes and lagoons that offer the
Minneapolis residents superb facilities for
recreation and relaxation. With two
excellent sandy beaches, wide, well-tended
lawns which are particularly good for sun-
bathing and evening cookouts, fishing and
boating, this fine lake area is popularly
appealing.

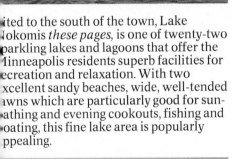

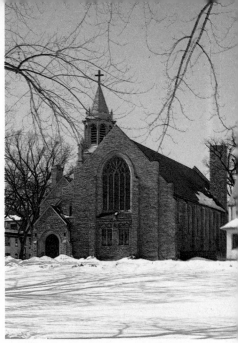

In beautiful Minnehaha Park *centre left,* set amid 144 acres of rolling woodland in south Minneapolis, are the majestic, cascading Minnehaha Falls *right,* immortalised by Longfellow in his famous poem "Song of Hiawatha". Flowing from its source at Lake Minnetonka, the crystal creek tumbles 53 feet in a powerful arch and joins the Mississippi River through a wooded gorge below the falls. Providing an excellent venue for various festivals, Minnehaha Park is the scene of the Swedish Festival's Svenskarnas Dag *top left,* held in June.

One of the most popular of the Minneapolis lakes, lovely Lake Calhoun *bottom left and below,* is also the largest and has three of the city's eleven public beaches. A particular feature of the lake are the paddle wheel excursion boat trips, which, in addition to half-hour cruises, make special three-lake tours and include Lake Cedar and the Lake of the Isles, where the pretty Lutheran Church *above* is seen nestled amid a soft white blanket of snow.

The majestic State Capitol in St Paul *previous page* has been the centre of Minnesota State Government since 1905. Within its interior may be seen the superb Rotunda *above*, with a symbolic glass star set in brass on the marbled first floor; the exquisite Rotunda Dome *below*, the Supreme Courtroom *left*, and the House Chamber *above right*, with its beautifully ornamented ceiling *right*.

Shown floodlit by night *above* and from the fountain in the reflecting pool at the Veterans Service Building *right*, the acclaimed Capitol Building *below*, with one of the largest unsupported domes in the country, was created by Cass Gilbert. Often referred to as the "Gold Horses", the sculpture group at the base of the dome entitled "The Progress of the State", by Daniel Chester French and Edward Potter can be seen *left. Above left* is the interior through the centre of the building, and *overleaf* the Senate Chamber.

Stately St Paul, the dignified capital of Minnesota, has, like its "Twin City" Minneapolis, an exciting skyline that rises above the banks of the Mississippi River.

Pictured in varying moods, the city is outlined at dusk beyond the coloured, curving freeways *above;* from Robert Bridge by night *right;* over the I-94 Freeway *below;* in a winter scene *bottom left,* and during an electric storm *top and centre left and overleaf.*

Around the lovely, terraced city of St Paul, shown in the superb night view *overleaf*, can be seen the Civic Center *top left*, from Summit Hill; Rice Park and the Landmark Center *bottom left*, and the imposing City Hall and Courthouse *below*.

Modelled after the 19th century riverboats which once plied the powerful Mississippi River *above*, the Josiah Snelling *right* and Jonathan Padelford *centre left*, are stern-wheel motor vessels that provide special excursions around Fort Snelling.

The Minnesota Twins, seen in an action-packed game versus Milwaukee at the Metropolitan Stadium *these pages*, first boosted the baseball scene in 1961, when, as the former Washington Senators, they moved into the area.

Framed by an ice-blue sky on a clear winter's day, the sentinel-straight skyscrapers of Downtown St Paul tower over the snow-banked marina on the Mississippi River *overleaf*.

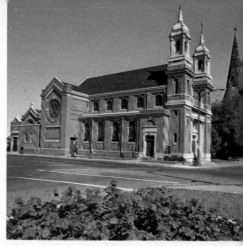

Included in the varied and exciting exhibits on display in St Paul's New Science Museum of Minnesota, is the skeleton of the Triceratops *top left*, a genus of large plant-eating dinosaur, and the replica of a traditional Maya dwelling *centre left*, whilst the Sears Roebuck Exhibition *bottom left* is part of a series of exhibits depicting the state's historical development in the Minnesota Historical Society *below*.

Constructed of St Cloud granite, the Cathedral of Saint Paul *below*, with its majestic interior *right*, was the creation of Emmanuel L. Masqueray who also designed the Baroque-towered St Louis Church on Cedar Street *top*.

As storm clouds gather over the dome of St Paul *overleaf*, a rainbow arch lights up the city skyline during an electric storm.

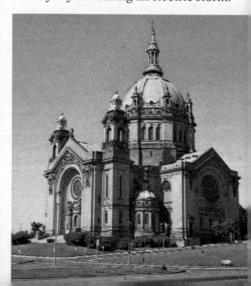

First published in 1979 by Colour Library International Ltd.
© Illustrations and text: Colour Library International (U.S.A.) Ltd, 163 East 64th Street, New York 10021.
Colour separations by La Cromolito, Milan, Italy.
Display and filmsetting by Focus Photoset, London, England.
Printed by Cedag bound by Eurobinder, Barcelona, Spain
Published by Crescent Books, a division of Crown Publishers Inc.
Library of Congress Catalogue Card No. 79-51719
CRESCENT 1979